ON THE
MASTER'S TIME

PAIGE COOPER

ILLUSTRATED BY MARY MOLLY SMITH

On the Master's Time

Illustrated by Mary Molly Smith.

ISBNs: 979-8-9908133-0-4 (Paperback)

         979-8-9908133-1-1 (Ebook)

Printed in the United States of America.

The Lord is good to those who wait for Him, to the soul who seeks Him. It is good that one should hope and wait quietly for the salvation of the Lord.

Lamentations 3:25-26

May this be a weapon in the hands of the woman who waits.

Acknowledgements

To my mom, thank you for always being in my corner. Thank you for never letting me settle for anything less than God's plan. Without your prayer and fasting, who knows where I may have ended up.

To my dad, thank you for telling me to dream. Thank you for pushing me to be who God has called me to be. Thank you for being my rock.

To my siblings, all of my in-laws, aunts, uncles, and grandparents, thank you for every seed of wisdom planted throughout the years. Thank you for taking time to sow into my life and support me. I treasure every word of encouragement and every piece of advice.

To my husband Sam, thank you for being so strong and steady, for being exactly who I needed in my life. Thank you for believing in me no matter what I set out to do, and for praying with me every step of the way. You were truly the missing piece of my puzzle.

To my mother-in-law and father-in-law, thank you for backing me, encouraging me, and being a listening ear.

You have never made me feel like an "in law," but just another daughter.

To my sister-in-law Mary, thank you for every drawing you have done. Thank you for the sacrifice of pushing yourself even when you were hurting, for working while you waited on the Lord to fulfill his promises to you. I believe through your obedience, God will pour out a blessing that you cannot contain.

And last but never least, thank You, Jesus, for entrusting me with this book. Thank You, Lord, for using me, even though I am unworthy. Thank You for never abandoning me, even when I walked away from You. Thank You for keeping every promise You made and giving me more than I could've dreamed. Thank You for turning my mourning to dancing and giving me beauty for ashes. No amount of words can express my gratitude for all that You have done, and all that You are still doing.

I know *You now* as the Promise Keeper.

Contents

Preface

To everything there is a season, a time for every purpose under heaven: a time to be born, and a time to die; a time to plant, and a time to pluck what is planted; a time to kill, and a time to heal; a time to break down, and a time to build up; a time to weep, and a time to laugh; a time to mourn, and a time to dance; a time to cast away stones, and a time to gather stones; a time to embrace, and a time to refrain from embracing; a time to gain, and a time to lose; a time to keep, and a time to throw away; a time to tear, and a time to sew; a time to keep silence, and a time to speak; a time to love, and a time to hate; a time of war, and a time of peace. What profit has the worker from that in which he labors? I have seen the God-given task with which the sons of men are to be occupied. *He has made everything beautiful in its time.* Also, He has put eternity in their hearts, except that no one can find out the work that God does from beginning to end (Ecclesiastes 3:1-11).

S easons. The worldly calendar claims there are four: Winter, Spring, Summer, and Fall. But in our walk as Christians there are many more and they aren't dictated by days or months. A season could be a full calendar year, or it could be a few weeks. A season in your life could last longer than you'd like it to, and some go by too fast. I've always been one to rush the season of life that I'm in. My dad has always said to me, "Daughter, don't wish your life away," meaning, "Don't waste the moment you're in, trying to get to the next." Because as we all know, you can't get moments back.

But growing up was the most exciting idea to me. I couldn't wait to turn 16, then 18, and then 20. Not even realizing that I wasn't enjoying the time I'd been given to the fullest. See, I've always looked too far ahead, or "put the cart before the horse," and I didn't really look around and thank God for where I was. The Lord has been so good to me, and my goal is to encourage you to stop, look around, and enjoy the adventure in every season. Count it all joy, and never stop thanking Him along the way. The promises of God will never return void. Yet it's easy to want to control the spiritual time frame and get disappointed when we think things *should* have happened by now. But I'm going to burst your bubble and remind you—your timing and God's aren't the same. See, the Bible says, "One day is as a thousand." Our mere seconds are eternity to God, and vice versa. So why do we think we can give Him deadlines or control His schedule? Imagine how He must laugh when we throw time into our prayers: "God, I need You to give me a husband before

I'm 20. But make sure he's all of these things." And we give God our list of demands.

Now, I'm not discouraging having specific prayers. I know the importance of the little details, and so does God. But we forget about surrendering to His perfect will and submitting ourselves to His perfect timing. Instead of planning everything out yourself and trying to accomplish things the way you think is best, remember that He already has everything mapped out. He knows the very day and hour that the very thing you're waiting for is coming. He has handwritten a specific story just for you. Jeremiah 29:11 says, "For I know the thoughts that I think toward you, saith the Lord, thoughts of peace, and not of evil, to give you an expected end" (KJV). The moment you accept in your spirit that God is in control and it is going to turn out the way He intends it to, you allow Him to give you a peace about your future and you can truly walk confidently. Trusting that He has made everything beautiful in *His* time.

CHAPTER 1

Wait Well, While Waiting at the Well

To be completely honest with you, my entire life I have struggled with submitting to God's will. I used to change the station and get angry when the song "Thy Will" would play. I would get mad when people told me to stop asking for what I wanted and just ask for His will to be done. I have battled with control issues and anxiety over my future. I found myself lying on the floor staring at the wall because I had no clue where my life was going, who I was going to marry, or what the possibility was that God would send me someone I didn't have to settle for. I would worry and panic with every month that I couldn't see the hand of God moving in my life. If I didn't have it all figured out, I would spiral into fear and sadness. I allowed the enemy to tell me it was never going to happen, and I was going to wind up alone.

To elaborate, a while back, I felt completely isolated. All of my friends and peers had married, moved away, and moved on with life. I was the last person left in our group. I felt as though God had forgotten me or that I had done something wrong to prolong my wait. Maybe I was being punished? But unbeknownst to me, while I may have lacked physical companionship, God was closer to me than ever before. The time I would've spent going out with my friends, I now spent in prayer and study. The time I would've spent on the phone to someone, I was interceding for my lost loved ones and for girls in similar situations to mine. God had me separated, not isolated. Even Jesus had to get alone for a while, away from the crowd. The times that the enemy tried to convince me were "awful" were the times God was doing a greater work in my life and establishing a faith in me that couldn't be shaken. God was teaching me empathy and grace. I was now able to see the hurt and pain in other people's lives, and I was able to witness to them the goodness of God. The Lord had me alone for a reason. The enemy tried to lie to me, telling me that it was punishment. But instead, God whispered empowerment.

During these times of drought, the biggest lie the enemy sells you in your waiting season is loneliness. If you buy it, you will find yourself isolated and tormented with depression and hopelessness. For the longest time I believed I was going through my trials alone, and nobody cared or understood how I felt. The enemy plays on your emotions and will use them against you. However, you have to keep things in perspective and keep your emotions under subjection. Ecclesiastes says there is a time to weep; thus, God gave you feelings for a reason. But He didn't intend for your feelings to rule your life. So every day we must make the choice to crucify our flesh, our wants and desires, and even our emotions.

> Trust in the Lord with all thine heart; and
> lean not unto thine own understanding. In
> all thy ways acknowledge him, and he shall
> direct thy paths (Proverbs 3:5-6 KJV).

The Bible says the heart is deceitfully wicked above all things. This is why the world tells you to follow your heart. Because if you're always relying on feelings, you're less likely to use discernment and allow the Holy Spirit to guide your life. The gift of discernment is arguably the most important one to have. It's like a spiritual traffic light telling you when to go and when to stop. It tells you when to move forward and when to turn in a different direction. The Holy Spirit brings discernment when you allow Him into your life. If you tune your ear to hear Him, He will lead and guide you through the winding paths of emotions and misunderstandings and he'll bring you exactly where you're supposed to be.

For example, there were times I would convince myself that someone was right for me or that they were the one God had promised when in reality I was cutting corners out of impatience. I would accept counterfeit versions of the promise, similar to the Abraham with Ishmael and Isaac scene. I found myself in a situation in which I knew I was in disobedience to the Lord. As a warning He gave me a dream. One night, as I slept, I imagined it was my wedding day. One by one every aspect of the event was falling apart and failing. The venue I had booked, had booked another wedding on top of ours. So I rearranged the location; instead, I planned to have our wedding on my granny and pop's property (which had already been sold, she had passed away years prior). Continuing on, my bouquet disintegrated in the box and in my dream I said, "It's okay, I'll go pick a new bouquet from Pop's landscape." Then when we opened the closet, my veil had been eaten with moths and my dress had burn marks as if someone had taken lit cigarettes to my train. At the end, the groom never showed up, and it began to rain. I woke with the emptiest, darkest feelings. This confirmed I was not walking in God's will for my life.

Some time passed and one afternoon I was having coffee with a great woman of God. Out of nowhere she looked at me and said, "You need to stop trying to pick your own bouquet!" I was in shock. I had not shared a single detail of that dream with her. This was a wakeup call. I knew exactly what she meant: stop trying to control your own destiny.

All along I had been denying the gift of discernment, but after my dream I could no longer ignore the voice of the Lord clearly telling me "No." As much as it hurt me to deny my feelings and obey the Lord, I knew He had a plan that was greater than mine.

When I finally let go of *all* of my expectations, I stopped trying to fit God into *my* plan. Instead, I started asking Him to fit me into *His* plan. This is when I experienced true peace and comfort knowing His ways were better than mine.

> For my thoughts are not your thoughts, neither are your ways my ways, saith the Lord. For as the heavens are higher than the earth, so are my ways higher than your ways, and my thoughts than your thoughts (Isaiah 55:8-9 KJV).

When I finally gave up on trying to figure it all out, I realized that there were beautiful things happening in the moments I usually discarded as "dry seasons." Those times when I couldn't see God moving, it was because He was working things out that I didn't even see coming. He was fighting for me behind the scenes and orchestrating everything to fall into place.

God is always working for you even when you feel like He's nowhere to be found. In the darkest and loneliest moments of your life, He is standing right beside you. Sometimes the Lord is silent to test your faith and your patience. When the storm arose on the sea and Jesus was asleep, the disciples panicked and questioned whether or not He cared if they perished. We do the same thing. The moment it starts to storm, we question His presence in our lives. But I have good news for you. He has never left you, not even once. And He promises that He never will. Those times when you feel like absolutely nothing is happening and nothing good could come from it, these are the times when the most work is being done in you.

When you plant a seed in the ground, you bury it. The seed is enclosed in total darkness and it's alone. From your perspective, nothing seems to be happening. But what you can't see is beneath the surface of the ground, that seed is breaking open, and its roots are beginning to sprout. The breaking of the seed is what brings forth life. That seed is growing and it's getting a firm root system, so that when the plant breaks the surface and springs upward, it won't be plucked up or moved easily. Roots are the most important part of a plant, and yet most of the time you can't see them. The roots are what carry nutrients and water to the plant, sustain it, and give it life.

When you allow yourself to be planted and rooted in your walk with the Lord, you are allowing Him to sustain you and bring you what you need daily. So maybe all you need in the "dark" season is a change of perspective. In the dark is where you learn to handle trials and refurbish the attitude you have toward them. These are the roots. And this will determine how healthy a plant you become. Will you be ready when the harvest comes? Look at this season as a steppingstone into the promised land. The trials you face in your waiting will shape you into the woman God you're called to be. The key to your breakthrough is your perspective and how you act in the waiting. Wait well, while waiting at the well!

She is not you and you are not she,
there are things that you just don't see.
Behind the scenes life is different,
a good front is placed on the internet.
Picture perfect and edited great,
filtered out is the bitterness and hate.
Compare and compete, you play the devil's game,
he wants carbon copies and everyone the same.
You were created to be a one of a kind,
a masterpiece of God's own design.
Envy crept in while you were scrolling,
Jealousy followed it, now it's controlling.
She is not you and you are not she,
but now you hate her
this was not the way it was supposed to be.
Wide is the gate that leads to destruction,
Social media has caused great corruption.
Shine your light and kindle your flame,
don't fall for the trap and play the devil's game.
You are not she, and she is not you,
Turn off your phone and do what you were called to do.
Look in the mirror and examine the reflection,
check your heart too, give it a good inspection
Make sure you don't find hate and strife,
jealousy and envy will cost you your life.

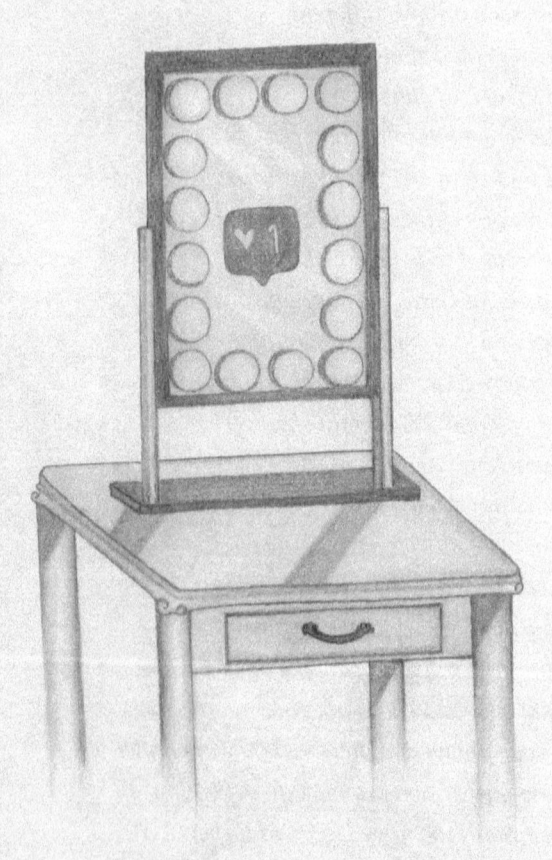

CHAPTER 2

The Dangers of Comparison

Have you ever found yourself scrolling through social media, and you see people living their "best lives," and you start to compare your life to theirs? You start picking yourself apart, thinking things like, "She's thinner than me," "I'll never be as talented as she is" or maybe even "I'll never have a marriage like that." One by one you go down the line and compare every aspect of yourself to someone's social media life that they have perfectly curated. They have added in the beauty and deleted the ugly to deliver the artificial "perfect" appearance. Our generation has filtered, photoshopped, and edited their lives and bodies to fit the standards of the internet. The reality is blurred, the truth is cropped out, and only the glittering highlights remain. Social media is a lie. No one's life is perfect, no one wakes up with a perfect blowout and a full face of makeup, no one's relationship is perfect, and no one's home is always that clean! The enemy wants you to be so blinded by comparison that you don't remember to shine the way God created *you* to shine! If he can distract you with what you don't have and make you envy your friends' lives, then he can get you to take your eyes off of the Lord's goodness and steal your joy.

> You shall not covet your neighbor's house;
> you shall not covet your neighbor's wife,
> nor his male servant, nor his female servant,
> nor his ox, nor his donkey, nor anything that
> is your neighbor's (Exodus 20:17).

When you are comparing your life to someone else's, you may find yourself coveting. To covet is to yearn to possess or have something. When you covet your neighbor, you are operating in jealousy. Comparison leads to jealousy, otherwise known as envy. Envy is a feeling of discontented or resentful longing aroused by someone else's possessions, qualities, or luck. If left to its own devices, feelings of envy will grow into deep roots of bitterness, then hatred.

Once hatred sets in, social media then tries to capitalize on your insecurities. It tells you you're not thin enough and promotes plastic surgeries. Then it tells you you're not curvy enough and promotes more plastic surgeries. Influencers and companies want to make a profit off your lack of confidence. Social media programs will make you to feel less than, but God disagrees with the world. He says you are more than enough.

It's not uncommon to feel envy, jealousy, bitterness, and even hatred toward yourself as you scroll through your social media feed. But don't let these feelings strangle your happiness and joy. Keep your eyes on what God is doing in your life.

We have to remember we are all in different seasons in our walk with the Lord. In each of these seasons, God is at work in different ways. Some are in a seemingly barren season of Winter, when the work is being done underground. Some are in the season of Spring, when you plant seeds and start to see things blossom. Some are in Summer, enjoying the fruits of their labors, and some are in Fall, the time of harvest and rest. You don't ever see the preparation people had to put in to get where they are now. You don't see the tears shed during the sleepless nights in prayer. You don't see the meals pushed aside during times of fasting for that promise. You don't see the battles they faced. You don't see the road they had to walk to get to their promised land. Don't envy their celebrations; instead, ask about their trials. Most importantly, don't limit what God is able to do. If He did it for them, He can do it for you!

Stop, take a deep breath, and look around at all of the things God has blessed you with! Look at the talents and gifting that He gave you! God created you in his image; you are fearfully and wonderfully made.

> I will praise You, for I am fearfully and wonderfully made; marvelous are Your works, and that my soul knows very well (Psalm 139:14).

Social media programs the need for constant validation. It makes you believe you need a certain number of
likes or comments in order to be worthy. I'm here to tell
you that no matter what your social media standing is,
there is One greater who believes you are worthy enough
to die for. He loves you so much that He gave his life for
you! Jesus was perfect, sinless, and pure, and yet He was
among the most hated. Your ultimate goal is to reflect
Him. So don't be discouraged or think less of yourself
based on who "likes" your photos. Your value comes from
your Creator.

> If the world hates you, you know that it
> hated Me before it hated you. If you were
> of the world, the world would love its own.
> Yet because you are not of the world, but
> I chose you out of the world, therefore the
> world hates you (John 15:18-19).

We should be more concerned about what our heav-
enly Father thinks of us. The Bible says to be a friend of
the world is to be an enemy with God. When you live
according to trends and worldly standards, you slowly
become less like Him and more like the world. The world
will tell you that you don't have to be the gender you
were assigned at birth, that you can identify as whatever
you want to be and marry whatever gender pleases you.
Everything the world promotes is in direct disobedience
and rebellion to the word of God. If you are not grounded
and confident in your identity in Christ, the world will

attempt to sway you and change who you are. We need to focus on His standard of holiness rather than the world's standard of trendiness. The world's trend is provocative and ever changing. But the Lord says, "Be ye holy, as I am holy," and His truths are everlasting.

God sees past the filters and looks at the heart. You can be outwardly pretty and inwardly awful. Bitterness will cause a beautiful person to become ugly. The comparison competition that comes from social media never benefits a woman of God.

How can you be who God called you to be if you're so busy competing with everyone else?

This was exactly my struggle.

Building on my example from the previous chapter, when I was in my waiting season, I too battled comparison. On social media, I would see other women who had what I was asking God for. As time crept on, this comparison grew into jealousy and bitterness toward those women. I couldn't be happy for my friends getting married because I was so wrapped up in what I didn't have. I would spend all of my time spectating everyone else's lives, *and I had forgotten to live my own*. Rather than enjoying the place I was in and deepening my walk with the Lord, I froze and became bitter. My bitterness made me unusable to the Lord. It took finding an altar of repentance and asking Him to take my heart of stone and replace it with a heart of flesh (Ezekiel 36:26) to be able to come out of that clouded mindset.

When I finally deleted all the social media apps, this helped me to stop focusing on everyone else's lives, and I began to enjoy my own. I no longer cared what people thought, and there was no rush to be like someone else. I could now be truly happy for everyone around me, including myself. The scales fell from my eyes, and I was able to thank God for the blessings He had given my friends. And I thanked Him for what I knew He would do for me. It brought me true contentment. I stopped dealing with hatred, bitterness, and judgment, because I was no longer subject to seeing everything everyone else did. Sometimes, getting offline and looking around at the blessings in your life can keep you grounded. And maybe there is someone out there who envies the life God has given you. Be grateful. You don't have to compare.

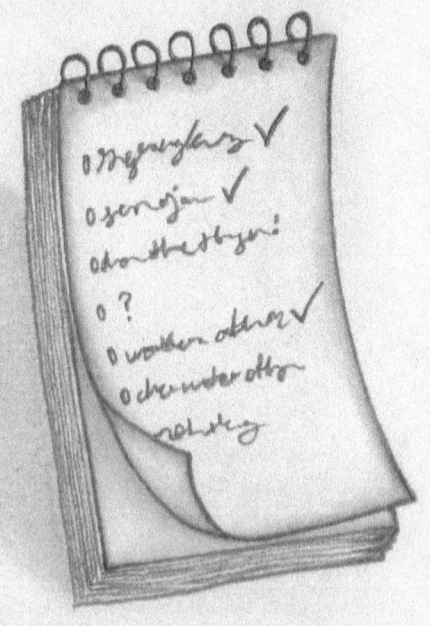

CHAPTER 3

Confirmation or Conformation?

Confirmation, or conformation? This is the question you should ask yourself when something is spoken over or into your life. We often call this "a word." A "word" can be a word of encouragement, a word of wisdom, a word of warning, or a word of prophecy. A word of encouragement can bring you hope in a time of despair. A word of wisdom can bring instruction at a time of decision. A word of warning can keep you from walking out of God's will. But a word of prophecy could be speaking something that has not happened yet. When a word of prophecy is spoken over your life, you must make sure it is confirmation and not conformation.

To *confirm* is to establish the truth or correctness of something previously believed, suspected, or feared to be the case. Confirming something brings clarity and validation. Conforming is almost the opposite. To *conform* is to comply with rules, standards, laws, or beliefs. To conform is to change something to make it fit to something else;

often it is your own desires. Interestingly enough, when you search for the definition of the word *conform*, it says that it is sometimes confused with *confirm*.

So often we don't truly want to hear what God is saying to us; we just want what He says to line up with what *we want*. Your own desires can cause you to "conform" or change a word to fit your own agenda. You have to take a spoken word and compare it to *the Word*. What does *the Word* say about it? The results should align. Many times, as women we seek "a word" so desperately in prayer, and yet we forget we have a book filled with God's direct words! Sometimes you can be seeking for the wrong reason. You can't expect God to tell you exactly what you want to hear. Often the answer is no, and sometimes the answer is the opposite of what we expected. You must be careful not to have "itching ears," filtering in only what *you want* to hear.

> For the time will come when they will not endure sound doctrine, but according to their own desires, because they have itching ears, they will heap up for themselves teachers; and they will turn their ears away from the truth, and be turned aside to fables (2 Timothy 4:3-4).

The Lord will use people under a prophetic anointing to speak into your life. In my walk I had many things spoken into my life. Some came to pass and some I haven't seen fulfilled yet. Sometimes I sought a word to fit my own wants and desires and was met with a hard "no." There were times a word was spoken into my life and I tried to mold it like play dough to fit the situation. Like trying to place a square into a triangle, I wanted it to fit but it didn't because it wasn't God's will.

Sometimes something can be spoken that your spirit doesn't resonate with. If you are walking in discernment, the Holy Spirit will give you the ability to know what is of God and what is not. When a word is spoken from the Lord, it will be confirmed. You must carefully pray about a "prophetic" word spoken over you. Pray that the Lord would confirm it in your spirit, whether by direct Holy Spirit confirmation or by someone else speaking confirmation. It is crucial to pray fervently about a prophetic word to make sure that it lines up with the Bible and it lines up with the true character of God.

> Quench not the Spirit. Despise not prophe-
> syings. Prove all things; hold fast that which
> is good (1 Thessalonians 5:19-21 KJV).

In his book *Thus Saith the Lord?* John Bevere writes, "Telling the people what they want to hear at the expense of what they need to hear weakens the church. It causes people to seek the gifts and manifestations to the neglect of pursuing the character of God."[1]

When I first read this, it shook me to my core and caused me to search my heart. I was led to repent for the

---

1. *Thus Saith the Lord?* (Lake Mary, Florida: Charisma House, 1999), 34.

times I only went to a service in search of the prophetic manifestations instead of the presence of the Lord and His voice. As I matured in my walk with the Lord, I stopped seeking for "a word" and started digging in *the Word* to further my relationship with Him.

I want to ask you some questions I wish someone would've asked me long ago: Do you truly want to know Him, or do you just want to have a blueprint of your future? Are you seeking Him to know Him, or are you only in it for what He can do for you? Are you seeking His presence or His presents? Is He your priority or are you your priority? It's easy for us to develop a sense of tunnel vision and think me, me, me. As a result, this may cause us to grow stale in our relationship with him. We only ever think to ask for things for ourselves, like a mate, and a perfected one at that. We stop asking for things for others, like miracles in our families or open doors in ministry or opportunities to spread the Gospel. We only see Him as a servant or genie or a matchmaker, not the Master and Creator. Sure, it's not wrong to ask the Lord to provide a godly husband, loving children, and a nice house, but is that all you're concerned about?

> But seek ye first the kingdom of God, and
> his righteousness; and all these things shall
> be added unto you (Matthew 6:33 KJV).

My goal is not to diminish the importance of the prophetic ministry, but to show you how to take it to the Lord. Ask Him to confirm it to you, and make sure you aren't twisting and conforming the word to fit your own desires. John Bevere also wrote, "Has the Holy Spirit been reduced to a fortune teller who performs in order to maintain a crowd?"[2] Carefully examine the intention behind a spoken word. Make sure it isn't conformed by the speaker to tell you what you want to hear. Sometimes a word is spoken out of the goodness of someone's heart and may be what they want to see blossom in your life, but it may not be truth. It is important to have the gift of discernment to be able to know the difference between the true and the false.

> Beloved, believe not every spirit, but try the spirits whether they are of God: because many false prophets are gone out into the world (1 John 4:1 KJV).

---

2. *Thus Saith the Lord?* (Lake Mary, Florida: Charisma House, 1999), 33.

CHAPTER 4

Pressed to Perfection

Time. Sixty seconds in a minute. Sixty minutes in an hour. Twenty-four hours in a day. Seven days in a week. Four weeks in a month. Twelve months in a year. Earthly time is precise and significant. God's timing is similar with significance, but not in structure. As humans we are on a constant time-sensitive schedule. There are specific times we eat, specific times we go to church, specific times we work, specific times to wash our hair even. We live by a schedule, and that's good—it helps us to stay productive and organized. *But* we have to be reminded He is *not* on our schedule.

I've found myself completely unable to sleep some nights, no matter what I do. I would toss and turn and cry out of exhaustion, and then I would hear that still small voice urging me to press in. See, I hadn't made time for Him all day, and now at four o'clock in the morning God was requiring it of me to open my Bible and hear what He had to say. We get so busy and preoccupied with our own desires that we forget to just bask in His presence.

The Lord's timing is unfathomable to our minds. Sometimes it just doesn't make any sense. We see a situation in which we *need* Him to move, and we expect it to be done as soon as we ask. God is not a genie in a bottle. His answer may not come as soon as we want it to, but that does not mean He doesn't hear us. If you have been praying for something for what seems like an eternity, press on. Delay is not denial; delay builds faith. You must have faith in order to wait for a promise to come to pass. If you order food at a restaurant and it takes longer than usual to come out, does that mean you should get up and leave? Or do you have the patience to wait on what you asked for? Timing is everything. If God had given me what I was praying for when I thought He should've, I wouldn't have been ready for it! Some things take preparation. While you are in the midst of a waiting season, focus on what God is trying to teach you or do in your life while you wait.

If David had gone to the palace the moment he was anointed to be king, he wouldn't have had the preparation that shepherding gave him. God allowed him to face trials, which grew his character and prepared him for his future. He conquered the bear and the lion. This perseverance established the confidence he needed to face Goliath. As a result, he became a great leader and defended his people the way he defended his sheep. Thus, in this season his outward appearance was just that of a shepherd boy, but inwardly he was being made into a king. The anointing was instant, but the position took time! God had it all planned out. It is the same for you and I.

> But, beloved, do not forget this one thing,
> that with the Lord one day is as a thou-
> sand years, and a thousand years as one
> day (2 Peter 3:8).

He knows exactly when to deliver what He's promised you. While I was in my waiting season, God was equipping me with the spiritual weapons I would need in order to walk into the promised land. He equipped me with a strong prayer life that would lead to a fruitful marriage and ministry. Here He taught me to "pray without ceasing" even when the answer wasn't coming. And while facing disappointment and doubt, God equipped me with boldness to stand in the face of the enemy and take authority over my life and my home. Additionally, He gave me the strength to push aside my feelings and continue doing what He called me to do, such as ministering in my church and to a group called "Girls in the Waiting" on a specific social media platform. This all taught me that I did not have to be married in order to be used for the Kingdom.

Every promise comes with the enemy creeping not far behind. You can always expect the enemy to move when God moves. The devil will come in and whisper lies to make you grow weary and to question or doubt the move of God in your life. He'll come in and try to snuff you out before you can receive the promises of God. Keep your eyes on Jesus as you're waiting and don't fall for the traps set by the enemy. Trials and tribulations will come in life, but pray through them. Ask God to equip you with spiritual weapons that will help you conquer the attacks of the enemy!

> My brethren, count it all joy when you fall into various trials, knowing that the testing of your faith produces patience. But let patience have its perfect work, that you may be perfect and complete, lacking nothing (James 1:2-4).

When you take an olive and you press it, you get oil. But it's not as simple as that.

You see, in order to get oil, that olive needs to be ripe. It needs to be in perfect condition to be able to produce high quality oil. In ancient Israel, when an olive had reached ripeness, it was first lightly pressed to produce a sweet, thin oil. The remaining olives, which varied in ripeness, were pressed with a heavier weight. Inferior oil was made from olives that were stored longer until they had softened. Others may have been left in pits underground to make them sweat until they were ready.

Oil is not cheap, and real anointing doesn't come without time and pressing. Your anointing can only be authentic if you've been through some hard things. An anointing is the manifested presence, approval, and favor of God resting upon someone. It is when the Holy Spirit is directly involved in the situation. The anointing can rest upon a person, thing, or event.

At other times, oil is used to physically represent the spiritual event of anointing. David was physically anointed with oil when he was to become king, and that represented the favor of God resting upon him. He had the anointing resting on his life that made him able to slay Goliath. You see, the anointing takes you where talent and education cannot. You can be "effective" without it, but when the favor of God is upon your life, you soar, and no man can stop you. However, obtaining the anointing isn't just pouring oil on your head, it stems from a life of seeking the face and presence of God. When you spend time in His presence, the Holy Spirit will rest upon you.

> And John bore witness, saying, "I saw the Spirit descending from heaven like a dove, and He remained upon Him. I did not know Him, but He who sent me to baptize with water said to me, 'Upon whom you see the Spirit descending, and remaining on Him, this is He who baptizes with the Holy Spirit'" (John 1:32-33).

The anointing can also be explained as the Holy Spirit coming upon you for a divine purpose. In Luke 4:18, Jesus reads, "The Spirit of the Lord is upon me," and continues to tell of the task at hand. Further, at the beginning of Luke 4, Jesus was tempted in the wilderness by satan. He was in the midst of a trial. He was pressed by the enemy to see if He really was who He claimed to be. When you and I are pressed, what's really inside comes out. The pressing will

39

prove whether or not the anointing is authentic. The pressing from trials may cast a shadow on an anointing, but God's anointing always triumphs. The anointing is what makes the difference.

Unripe olives are bitter. They are mostly unusable because they are too hard, but over time they become ready. In life sometimes you aren't ready to be used yet. You must remain a little longer, until your heart is softened and pliable in the hands of the Father. Then you will face hardship and trials as a sort of pressing, to produce the anointing in your life. Timing is everything. Sometimes miracles and answers are just not ready to be brought forth. Delay is not denial; wait on the Lord! Patience is a fruit of the Spirit, and that fruit is only useful once it is tested and mature.

If you've ever cooked with a cast iron skillet, you know that it must be "seasoned." When you season it, you take a little oil on a paper towel and wipe the entire pan to coat and seal it, preventing moisture from getting into the pan and creating rust. Then you put the cast iron skillet in your oven on a high temperature and bake the oil in. As Christian women, we need to be well seasoned to handle life. We must apply the oil (the anointing) and go through a little heat to produce something usable. If that pan wasn't seasoned, food would stick to it, rust would form, and it would be useless. Let us be patient through affliction as God guides us and makes us useful for His kingdom.

In this you greatly rejoice, though now for a little while, if need be, you have been grieved by various trials, that the genuineness of your faith, being much more precious than gold that perishes, though it is tested by fire, may be found to praise, honor, and glory at the revelation of Jesus Christ (1 Peter 1:6-7).

Your anointing is going to cost you greatly. Choose to allow the trials to make you and not break you. Without refining, gold is no good. Without pressing, there would be no oil. Without pressure, there are no diamonds! Precious things are born of pressure! The road won't be easy, but it will bring great reward.

Fall at My feet and call upon Me,
what you struggle with I've already seen.
You build and build this wall around your spirit and your heart,
but today, My daughter, it will fall.
Bricks of hatred bitterness and anger,
so heavy on your shoulders and you can't even see the danger.
You stack them high one by one,
until you've blocked yourself in
but today all comes undone.
It's time for a demolition,
wrecking and breaking down this heart condition.
I'll tear down strongholds and unlock the doors
that have held you in so long and can no longer be ignored.
I'll free you from every hurt and every struggle,
cleanse you and make you new
I'll turn you into a vessel that I can use.
I'll fill the cracks and unclog your heart,
As of now this is a new start.
This is a choice and it's yours to make,
Will you surrender your life and allow a clean break?
I'll refresh your mind and grant you peace,
just come to Me and fall on your knees.

CHAPTER 5

What are You Packing?

Have your parents ever told you that you needed an "attitude adjustment"?

Maybe you were being a little bratty, rude, or just had an overall rotten attitude? In my daily walk with the Lord, I have found myself needing an attitude adjustment at times. When my disposition was just awful and I was being a Debbie downer, I knew I wasn't in the right standing with the Lord. Do you find yourself being snarky or quick to say something nasty? Do you have days when you have a problem with everyone and everything? Maybe you need an attitude adjustment like I did.

During a certain point in my life, I allowed bitterness to creep in so deeply it began to eat away at my core. At the time, I barely noticed that I was walking around being mean, passing judgment, making horrible comments about people, and taking every opportunity to say something rude. As this pattern continued, I was lying in bed one night and the Holy Spirit reminded me of something my granny would say: "Beauty is skin deep, but ugly is to the bone." At that moment I knew I was being truly ugly and I had a useless attitude. As I reflected, I realized this frustration stemmed from resentment toward people who had what I wanted and other resentments stemming from unforgiveness I was unwilling to address. I was ashamed. I repented immediately and prayed that God would cleanse my heart and renew a right spirit within me. I realized it wasn't just my attitude that needed to change, but also my heart. Your heart pours out when your mouth opens. You can't hide something like bitterness; the moment you speak, it flows right out.

> A good man out of the good treasure of his heart brings forth good; and an evil man out of the evil treasure of his heart brings forth evil. For out of the abundance of the heart his mouth speaks (Luke 6:45).

When you plant an apple, you get an apple tree. When you plant oranges, you get orange trees. What you plant, you will grow. If you plant seeds of bitterness and anger, that is what you're going to reap.

Often, when a girl gets engaged, she starts to prepare. She buys a wedding dress, honeymoon clothes, housewares, new luggage—the list is endless. So much emphasis is placed on preparation in the natural, but what about in the spirit? In the natural you're whitening your teeth, tanning every day, working out so you look your best on your wedding day, but what condition is your heart in?

Have you stopped to prepare your spirit and your heart? Is your spirit pliable? Are you willing to prune your heart? If you aren't careful, things you refuse to address and get rid of now will be dragged into your promised land with you. The baggage you hold on to will be carried right along into the next season. I found that unresolved issues from my "single season," such as bitterness or unforgiveness, were carried into my marriage and became much harder to deal with. Don't drag that kind of baggage into your promised land; empty it at the feet of Jesus and leave it behind.

Marriage is not a picnic all of the time. When you have two imperfect people who become one, well, now you have double the trouble. If you face these battles incorrectly, you can damage your marriage. However, the more perfected we are in Christ, the better we are prepared to bring glory to God and honor to our husbands. As a result, our marriage will bloom beautifully.

Marriage is truly an offering; it's a sacrifice of the flesh. She does the extra load of laundry so he can finish his project for work. He gives up his last sip of coffee because he knows she loves it. She makes his lunch the night before because she knows how tired he is. He works a few extra hours to take her out to a nice dinner on Friday night. Love like this is poetic symmetry and is a little reflection of Jesus on the cross, sacrificing Himself for His bride, the church.

So in your waiting season, take the time to exercise your spirit in preparation for marriage. You will need unending amounts of patience, peace, and meekness. You will need to be able to hold your tongue and submit your feelings to the Lord. If you are like me, this might be a little difficult, but it is required of you. You will need to apologize, even when you don't think you've done anything wrong. Marriage is hard work, and you must be well prepared to know how to deal with its unexpected challenges.

> But the fruit of the Spirit is love, joy, peace, longsuffering, kindness, goodness, faithfulness, gentleness, self-control. Against such there is no law (Galatians 5:22-23).

Check your fruit! It won't be a one-time thing; daily we must examine ourselves. You must carry all the fruits of the Spirit with you into marriage. As you pack and prep for the next phase of life, ask the Lord to show you your weaknesses so you have opportunities to strengthen them before due time. You need love to keep your marriage together when things get hard. You need joy so that your emotions aren't dependent on your husband because some days they aren't always happy. You need peace so that in the midst of chaos or arguments you can just apologize and walk away from it. You need longsuffering or patience when your husband is taking too long in the bathroom or he says something that hurts your feelings. You need kindness for the days you don't feel like being sweet, but you do it anyway. You need goodness in the midst of an evil world that impedes both of your lives. You need faithfulness in the day when marriage is no longer valued by people, and the enemy comes in to divide your home. You need gentleness to correctly care for your family. You need self-control to hold your tongue and build up your marriage rather than tearing it down. Each fruit is vital for a successful, loving marriage.

> Even so, every good tree bears good fruit, but a bad tree bears bad fruit. A good tree cannot bear bad fruit, nor can a bad tree bear good fruit. Every tree that does not bear good fruit is cut down and thrown into the fire. Therefore by their fruits you will know them (Matthew 7:17-20).

On days when I feel like I have failed or my fruit is rotting, I have learned to fall at His feet and ask Him to forgive me and make me new. As women, we set the emotional thermostat in our homes: we control the mood. If you are angry and snappy, it will affect your husband and your children. Nobody is perfect. There will be times when you are excelling in these areas and times when you fall short, but thankfully we know the Potter. All you have to do is ask Him to mold you and shape you again, like the potter with the clay.

Didn't I say?
Didn't I tell you I would?
Didn't I promise you all things good?
Haven't I assured you My word is true?
That everything I promised, I will give to you?
Don't you believe I am who I say?
I'm the one who granted you another day
I'm the one who healed your heart,
Who forgave you, cleansed you,
and mended the broken parts.
I called you, I chose you, I set you apart.
I separated you from the rest
I've brought you this far,
So why do you stress?
Trust Me daughter for My word will not fail
I know the plans I have for you,
down to every little detail.
Remember who you are
and who you're called to be,
Go out and do my work, and leave the rest to Me.
Do not grow weary, for in due time you will reap
Be patient, My daughter, My promises I will keep.

CHAPTER 6

The Weight of the Wait

Wait, what? What is waiting?

To wait is to stay where one is or delay action until a particular time or until something else happens. It also is defined as delaying action until someone arrives or is ready. On the other hand, weight is the heaviness of a person or thing. The wait carries a lot of weight. Whatever you are waiting on the Lord for can become heavy at times. It can feel like there is an elephant sitting on your heart and you're anxious to just push it off. Waiting can be so weighted that you feel deflated and hopeless after a while. The wait is a spiritual exercise; it is strengthening your faith, your trust, your patience, and your obedience. You lift physical weights, usually at the gym, in order to build muscle. They have something in common—can you see where I'm going here? You use different sized weights in different ways to target specific areas! It is the same in at the spiritual gym. We must exercise our spirit with waits as well. Waiting on the Lord builds the qualities necessary to obtain the promises. Obedience is crucial to your walk as a Christian. There are many cases in the Bible I which men and women did not wait well. So their disobedience and impatience caused a lot of chaos down the road. The Bible says obedience is better than sacrifice. But sometimes disobedience will lead to delay, denial, destruction, or even forfeit.

As an example, Adam and Eve's disobedience caused them to forfeit the original plan that God had for their lives. Moses' anger and disobedience caused him to be denied access into the promised land. The children of Israel's disobedience and complaining delayed their entrance into the promised land. King Saul's disobedience cost him his life and led him to forfeit his throne. Jonah's disobedience landed him in the belly of the big fish. Lot's wife's disobedience caused her body to be utterly destroyed.

When God tells you to wait for something, don't get ahead of Him and try to make things happen on your own. If God says "No" that means no! Don't pry open doors that God has slammed shut! If the Lord speaks a direct instruction to you, obey. Obey His voice and He will lead you where you need to be. Patience is one of the hardest values to obtain in life. We are living in the "microwave generation" where we just want everything now! Sometimes, we don't want to wait on what God has for us because we think it is taking longer than it should. And sometimes, we don't want to wait for what He has for us because we trust in our own abilities more than His. We only want His will if it's on our clock, and if He is not fast enough, well, we'll just do it ourselves. But this is the wrong attitude.

Patience is the capacity to accept or tolerate delay, trouble, or suffering without getting angry or upset. Are you walking in patience? You will need it. Additionally, faith is complete trust or confidence in someone or something. The Bible says faith is the substance of things hoped for, the evidence of things not seen. We know that without faith it is impossible to please God. But faith without works is dead, so you have to actively walk in faith! In order to wait properly, you must trust that He is working everything out. This means you need both patience and faith. When you trust Him fully, you don't need to have all the answers. You don't need to know who, what, where, when, and how. You just need to fully surrender and believe that He who has promised is faithful!

> Let us hold fast the confession of our hope
> without wavering, for He who promised is
> faithful (Hebrews 10:23).

There is an old saying that my family always uses: "It is better to wait long than to marry wrong." Impatience can't speed up the process, but it can lead you down roads you were never meant to go down. No amount of pushing, shoving, or forcing will expedite God's plan. You will just wear yourself out in the meantime. God's timing is impeccable. The Lord orchestrated my life beautifully, but it took time. There were pieces that God was moving and working on behind the scenes that I couldn't see. My husband came into my life at the perfect time, and the Lord has blessed me more than I deserved. But I had to wait for it. There were times I could've moved the chess pieces for God but would have interrupted God's perfect plan for my life.

My wait was not as long as some people's, but it was hard. The enemy would whisper lies that it was my fault I still wasn't married, or that I would never be happy in God's will, or that it would be boring and not what I wanted. Let me address those lies of the enemy today! My husband is everything I ever prayed for, everything I ever dreamed of, and everything I didn't think I could have. He is my best friend, he is my ministry partner, he pushes me toward the Lord instead of hindering my walk, he is the physical embodiment of every promise that God made to me! I made a list of all the qualities I wanted in a husband two years before God brought Sam into my life. I prayed for these qualities often and they were very specific prayers. When we were engaged, I sat down and reread that list. I couldn't believe my eyes: he was the exact match! God is faithful, and He writes the best love stories. He gave me someone I could serve Him with, and that was the most important thing to me.

If you are waiting on the Lord for something, don't fret. If you knew what He had in store, you would not question or stress about it.

> But those who wait on the Lord shall renew their strength; they shall mount up with wings like eagles, they shall run and not be weary, they shall walk and not faint (Isaiah 40:31).

While He has called you to wait patiently, this does not mean to sit idly. There is more for you to do in the wait than just sit twiddling your thumbs. There is purpose in the wait.

Don't grow stagnant or stale in this season. Go out and do the work of the Lord in the meantime. Practice the fruits of the Spirit. Take this time to earnestly seek His face and fall in love with His Word. Become a strong intercessor; pray more than you worry! The enemy wants you to believe you can't serve God until you're married. That is a lie! Your relationship with the Lord cannot be based on your marriage or your relationships with other people. This time in your life is crucial because it is a small window to focus on and build your true, Christlike character. Waiting will either make you or break you. You will either crack under the pressures of impatience and stumble away from the will of God, or you can allow God to prepare you and use this time to grow.

Waiting can become a burden. It can seem to weigh you down with fear, anxiety, worry, and stress. But if you lay it down and place the situation in God's hands, He will bring you peace and contentment and faith to know He is in control. His plans far exceed anything you could ever come up with. Once you understand that, you will shed the weight of the wait.

> Now to Him who is able to do exceedingly abundantly above all that we ask or think, according to the power that works in us (Ephesians 3:20).

CHAPTER 7

Don't Wait to Worship, Worship While You Wait

Confusing the enemy seems like an impossible task, because it seems he's always there ready to strike. What if I told you there is a sure-fire way to confuse the devil? Can you guess what it is? It's worship!

Praise and worship confuses the enemy when you praise in spite of the circumstance! Worship is a form of warfare because you're proclaiming God's goodness and giving honor to Him in the midst of hard situations. When you worship, you are telling the enemy, "I don't care how this situation goes, *my* God is worthy of every breath!" Second Chronicles 20 talks about how praise confuses the enemy and wins the battle. Why, though? Because praise takes the emphasis off of our circumstance and places all the emphasis on God. How can the enemy torment you with anxiety and stress if you're busy exalting the Lord? He can't! When you choose to worship rather than worry, the Holy Spirit steps in and brings peace. Have you ever been having a miserable day, but you took the time to get alone with God and worship Him, and you noticed your mood changed? When you set your heart to worship Him, it changes the atmosphere.

Paul and Silas were imprisoned in Acts 16. They were bound by chains in the deepest part of the prison, with no signs of being released any time soon. Verse 25 says, "And at midnight Paul and Silas prayed, and sang praises unto God: and the prisoners heard them." So no matter your circumstance, you should worship God! For all that He has done, He is always worthy to be praised. Let's look at what verse 26 says.

> And suddenly there was a great earthquake, so that the foundations of the prison were shaken: and immediately all the doors were opened, and every one's bands were loosed (Acts 16:26 KJV).

Praise is a key that literally unlocks prison doors! Not only were Paul and Silas free, their jailer and his family were saved! Praise and prayer are a deadly combination that the enemy can't stand.

Worship can bring walls down in your life. In Joshua 6, they were commanded to march around the wall of Jericho once a day for six days. On the seventh day they were commanded to march seven times, and on the seventh time to shout and blow their horns and the wall would fall flat. Worship tears down the enemy's strong-holds over your life. Praise your way out! When doubt and fear creep in to torment you, begin to worship. James 4:7 says, "Submit yourselves therefore to God. Resist the devil, and he will flee from you."

If you ignore the enemy and don't give in to his schemes but instead place all of your attention on God, you will find yourself winning more often than losing. I studied that the Bible mentions the word *praise* at least 216 times, and the word *worship* is mentioned at least 100 times. See the importance? When we reach heaven, worship will be all that we do. You might as well get used to it now! How could we not justify giving honor and glory to the God who created the world? How have we grown so stale and stagnant that we don't understand the importance of worship?

Let me remind you of a biblical story. There were three Hebrew children who knew how important it was to worship God and only God. They refused to bow to a man-made idol, and as punishment they were thrown into a fiery furnace. But little did the king know, *their King* was in the fire with them the whole time, protect-ing them. What are you focused on in exchange for your worship? What or who is compromising that alone time with the Master? Is it your boyfriend? Your spouse? Your phone? Are you placing these things above wor-ship? When we think of worship we think of singing a pretty song on the pulpit in front of a group of people.

While some are called to lead worship, we are all called to *worship*.

Worship is more than just a song. Worship is bowing in humility and reverent fear of an all-powerful, almighty God. Worship is submitting your life to be used and led by the Holy Spirit, even if that entails letting go of or sacrificing something. Worship is lying at the feet of Jesus and pouring out everything you have, like Mary's alabaster box. Worship is pushing back a meal when your flesh is hungry, knowing your spirit is gathering strength and discipline. Worship is getting off of social media and pulling out the Word. Worship is saying no to you and yes to Him. Worship is reverence, submission, and sacrifice.

> Therefore, I urge you, brothers and sisters, in view of God's mercy, to offer your bodies as a living sacrifice, holy and pleasing to God—this is your true and proper worship (Romans 12:1 NIV).

You might be wondering, "So what does worship have to do with waiting?" Well, when I was home in my single season, I found myself battling a lot of different enemies. I battled fear, doubt, anxiety, worry, comparison, questioning, and overall I battled the word *wait*. But as time went on and my circumstance hadn't changed, I learned one of the most vital weapons to have in my spiritual artillery was worship and praise. Worship helped me to stop focusing on what I didn't have yet and stop placing so much emphasis on the fact that I had to wait for it. Praise taught me to open my mouth and say, "Thank you."

I realized the need to praise the Lord for all that He had already done for me. I began to focus on how He had delivered me and saved my soul. I focused on the faithfulness of God in my family and how He had never let me down. As an example, they call my Pop Ted "miracle man" because he fell from an elevator while working and should have been killed or paralyzed but he fully recovered and is more active than most teenagers. He almost died from Covid-19 but the Lord restored his ability to breathe and healed him. There are countless other times God has spared his life and has proved His faithfulness. Additionally, both of my parents have lost siblings and parents and yet God has given them strength and peace beyond words. Through every storm something beautiful was birthed. When the enemy tries to surround us with grief and pain, we worship through it and God turns our sorrow into dancing.

I realized that once I worshiped through the frustrations, the mountain of anxiety was now just a hill. The ocean of fear was nothing but a puddle. The battle of worry was conquered. I stopped questioning and started living. I slept peacefully resting on the promises of God. I stopped comparing myself to other women who were already given what I was waiting for. Worship and praise were my breakthrough. Now I have what the Lord had promised to me, and I can thank Him even more, praise

Him a little louder, and never stop giving Him honor and glory for writing my story.

> I will praise You, O Lord, with my whole heart; I will tell of all Your marvelous works (Psalm 9:1)

If you wait to praise the Lord until He does what you're asking, you are allowing the enemy to rob you of joy, peace, and contentment. Don't wait to worship; worship while you wait.

CHAPTER 8

Where He Guides, He Provides

We have all heard of the name *Jehovah Jireh*, which means "the Lord will provide."

It came from the book of Genesis, when Abraham went up the mountain to sacrifice Isaac, and God provided a ram to sacrifice instead. Abraham was walking in obedience to the Lord, and God made a way. Another instance of provision in the Bible was manna. While the children of Israel were wandering the desert, God provided them with a portion of manna from heaven every day to meet their nutritional needs. The Lord knows exactly what to give you every day to sustain you. I call manna the provision before the promise. I truly believe where God guides, He provides. Meaning if the Lord is leading you, He will meet your needs. Often, manna is viewed in the sense of monetary needs, and that's fine. But I am referring to the spiritual provisions of manna in our lives today. See, God provided a ram for Isaac's life, but

He didn't stop there. God provided Rebekah. God doesn't just provide you with the gift of life, He gives you someone to spend it with. Manna is proof of the mindfulness of the Master toward His creation. We can often confuse God's silence with a lack of concern for us, when really it's just the opposite. He never sleeps; He is always working behind the scenes on your behalf.

> For the Lord God is a sun and shield: the Lord will give grace and glory: no good thing will he withhold from them that walk uprightly (Psalm 84:11 KJV).

Have you found yourself with a lack of peace concerning your future? I know I have in seasons past. I would toil with the fear of the unknown. I was always concerned whether or not I would like God's plan. In that season, the provision I needed was peace. Sometimes we are so busy striving for the promised land that we don't realize we are starving in the wilderness. You don't have to wait until you have what God promised you in order to have peace; you can walk in peace now. You don't have to wait for fulfillment to have joy; you should be walking in joy now. God is able and willing to provide you with everything you need, not just a husband or a baby. He provides peace, joy, comfort, faith, patience, wisdom, direction, favor, and anything else you may lack. If you are serving the Lord, you can have access to all of these things.

Furthermore, God doesn't want you to be miserable in the waiting season. In fact, that can be the very thing that holds you back from receiving. Being content in the season you are in is vital. God provided time after time for the children of Israel but all they did was murmur and complain. Their lack of contentment and trust kept them wandering in the desert. What was supposed to take eleven days took forty years because they despised the provision of the Lord. Be careful not to overlook or take for granted what God is trying to do in the wait, because it could set you back. Until you come to the place where the Lord is enough, you will not move forward.

Psalm 23 is an example of the direction and provision of God. It begins with, "The Lord is my shepherd; I shall not want." That verse tells us that God provides for all our needs, there is no lack. Verse 2 says, "He maketh me lie down in green pastures, he leadeth me beside the still waters." This proves that He is guiding and directing you every day, especially toward things that fulfill you. To further prove that, verse 3 says, "He restoreth my soul: he leadeth me in the paths of righteousness for his name's sake" (KJV).

God revitalizes you so you may carry out and fulfill His will for your life. By understanding and applying this to my life, God led me to a place of expectation. I was no longer waiting fearfully or worriedly. I was waiting excitedly yet patiently. When I reached that place, it wasn't long after that God brought my husband into my life. In times of waiting when I felt that lack of contentment or that fear rise up again, I would cling to scripture.

The Lord will perfect that which concerneth me (Psalm 138:8 KJV).

God is perfecting every little detail right now. He is molding and shaping you to be ready to receive what He has for you. Maybe God has already provided manna in your life, but you've lost the taste for it. Is His provision not enough? The Word says that He provided them with a portion of manna every day, enough to meet their needs. Have you been trying to store up the manna from yesterday? Every day we need to ask the Lord to search our hearts and provide where we lack. We can't survive on yesterday's goosebumps. We can't thrive off of yesterday's prayer. We need Him every day, and we must trust Him even when we lose patience for His answers. I'm sure the children of Israel wanted more than manna; they probably wanted a feast. But God knew what would sustain them at this point and gave them what they needed. You have to learn to accept today's provision. His provision today might not be the promise; instead, it may fertilize the fruits of peace and patience needed to get through tomorrow.

In my single season, God filled the void that only He could fill. He provided me a measure of faith to carry me through the wait. Now, in my marriage, every day He provides me with wisdom and strength to be a godly wife. The Lord is continuing to teach me when to hold my tongue and when to give my opinion. He gives me the strength to wake up and take care of my home to the best of my ability. God has shown me how to love my husband and how to release the desire for control to Him. With God we have to continue to be flexible as the learning is never over. But the promptings toward perfection can guide us toward renewal.

God has been so good to me. What I had in mind for my life was not what God had planned for me. My mind didn't have the ability to plan it as beautifully as He did. I had imagined a somewhat plain life for myself, just happy and healthy. In the back of my mind, I had fears that God's plan for me was to settle. But little did I know the plan He had for me was beyond my expectations. I now live in a beautiful home in a quiet country town; I serve the Lord in ministry with my husband, whom I have watched blossom in his calling. My husband is my best friend, we do everything together, he makes even the mundane seem like an adventure. He went above my expectations and gave me a husband who brings joy to my heart. As an example, I have a husband who sits outside and gazes at the stars with me because he knows how much I love them. In every season manna looks a little different, but it's never been stale. God is mindful of your heart's desires, and He knows where your life is going. God has not brought you this far to leave you in the desert. Let Him provide your every need. Let Him be your portion for today.

> The Lord is my portion, saith my soul; there-fore will I hope in him. The Lord is good unto them that wait for him, to the soul that seeketh him (Lamentations 3:24-25 KJV).

71

It can be scary to fully rely on God to meet your needs, whatever they may be. But there is no safer place for your needs to be than in the palm of His adoring hand. Waiting on God is the best place to be. There is no limit to what He can do if you surrender your plans to Him.

> The young lions lack and suffer hunger:
> but those who seek the Lord shall not lack
> any good thing (Psalm 34:10).

The Lord instructed the children of Israel at the end of Exodus 16 to take a portion of manna and store it in a jar so that the future generations could see and remember the provision in the wilderness. Take a minute and look at all of God's provision in your life. God is consistent; He never fails or forgets what He has promised. There is no room for doubt or fear where He is taking you, only faith and trust. You must remember what He has done and thank Him for what is to come!

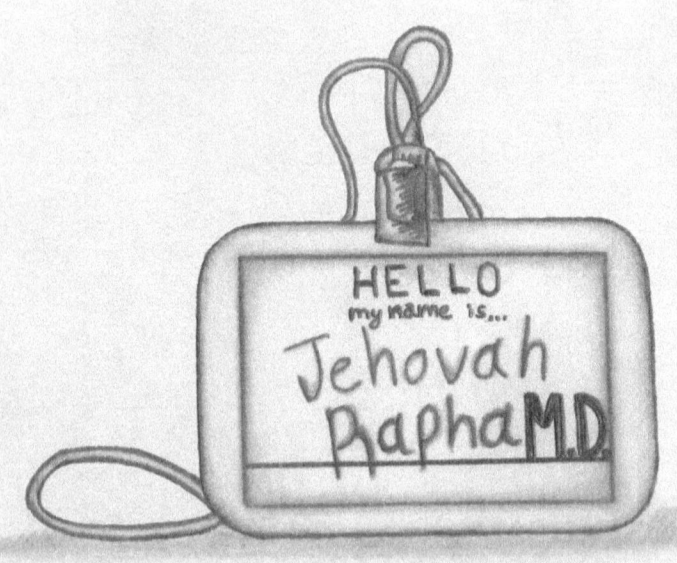

CHAPTER 9

I Need a Healer

Healing doesn't only apply to a physical need. Sometimes, it applies to an emotional need. For instance, you may need your broken heart healed. Or maybe it's mental and you may need your mind healed. We often talk ourselves out of asking God to heal us because we can't physically see the problem. Is your heart broken or hardened? Is your mind a constant battle-field? Maybe your need *is* physical. Have you received a report that man says is final? Is there a need in your body? Do you need a healing?

Then, my friend, you need to get in touch with Jehovah Rapha.

Jehovah Rapha is Hebrew for "the God who heals." Over and over again we see the miracle of healing take place in the Bible. We see lepers healed, we see barren wombs opened, we see the blind receive sight, we see lame people walking, we see people delivered from demons, we even see the dead brought back to life. But why is it when *we* need healing, it's somehow impossible?

How is it that we believe God is able to do it for everyone else but us? Why does our faith fall short when it comes to our own need? When we face a situation in which healing is needed, at first we seek the Lord and call on Him, but as time passes and the issue hasn't resolved, we start to question and doubt. Why?

Because the enemy knows that all it takes is faith the size of a mustard seed, and that situation can change in an instant. God has healed since the beginning of time; what would stop Him now? Does the Bible not say in Hebrews 13:8 that He is the same yesterday, today, and forever more?

Stop and ask yourself, "What areas of my life need to be healed?"

> But he was wounded for our transgressions, he was bruised for our iniquities; the chastisement of our peace was upon him; and with his stripes we are healed (Isaiah 53:5 KJV).

In both the Old Testament and the New Testament, healings take place. One of my favorite healings in the Bible was Naaman's, in 2 Kings 5:1-19. He had leprosy, an incurable disease. He traveled to Israel, to the prophet Elisha, to be healed. The story says that Naaman was instructed to dip in the Jordan seven times, and then he would be healed. But Naaman was annoyed at this, because he wanted to be healed instantly and he thought there were better ways. It wasn't until his servants came to him and asked him a very simple question that he changed his mind. Verse 13 says, "My father, if the prophet had told you to do something great, would you not have done it? How much more then, when he says to you, 'Wash and be clean'?" In the very next verse Naaman puts his flesh aside and does as he is told, and he is healed.

We act like Naaman sometimes. We feel as though God should heal us the way we want Him to, the second we ask. But God knows what He is doing, and He has a plan. Healing doesn't always come on our time, but that doesn't mean we stop asking. Another instance of healing was the woman with the issue of blood. Her illness had been going on for twelve years. Twelve years is 4,380 days. She had gone to doctors; she had treatments, and nothing changed—nothing until the day she met a man named Jesus. She knew if she could just touch Him, she would be made whole. When she touched Jesus, He felt power leave His body. He asked the crowd who touched Him, and the woman fearfully came forth. As she explained why she reached out to Him, He told her to go in peace, her faith had made her well (Matthew 9:20-22).

Her faith made her well. Sometimes the only thing that keeps us from receiving what we ask for is a lack of faith. In Second Kings 4, a barren woman comes to Elisha, and he tells her that this time next year she will have a son. She immediately responds with, "Don't lie to me." That woman was broken. She was bordering on hopelessness, and she had likely been disappointed many times in her waiting season. Verse 17 says, "But the woman conceived, and bore a son when the appointed time had come, of which Elisha had told her." She went from barren to blooming.

Yet another situation was when Jesus was visiting the pool in Bethesda. There was a lame man there who caught Jesus' eye. This man had been waiting for healing for a very long time.

> [He] had an infirmity thirty and eight years. When Jesus saw him lie, and knew that he had been now a long time in that case, he saith unto him, Wilt thou be made whole? (John 5:5-6 KJV).

When Jesus approached this situation, He asked the man one very simple question, "Will thou be made whole?" When something is whole, it is not missing anything; it's in favorable condition. It is lacking nothing.

> Jesus saith unto him, Rise, take up thy bed, and walk. And immediately the man was made whole, and took up his bed, and walked: and on the same day was the sabbath (John 5:8-9 KJV).

All it took was *His* word. He asked him if he would be made whole and then told him to get up and walk. That was the end—the man was healed of an issue he dealt with for *38 years*. In an instant, his life was changed.

Maybe this situation you're facing seems dead. Maybe the doctor has given you a final report. Maybe man has said, "It'll never happen." It could be hopeless. But do not forget there were multiple instances in the Bible when people had actually died and were brought back to life. There were bones that came together and formed a living, breathing army. Men were resurrected from death and stood on their feet again. There was even a man who was revived just by touching Elisha's bones. All Jesus had to do was send His word, and men lived again. No circumstance is ever dead. God is always more than able to heal and change the situation.

From the moment I formed your heart I declared it to be Mine,
Days weeks and years I worked on it,
I sat patiently and created the intricate design.
I built a heart that would chase after Me,
I stamped it with My signature, My very own decree.
A daughter I love enough to tell no,
She will seek My will only
And won't be satisfied with the status quo.
My daughter was created with a purpose and a vision,
She presses on without doubt
Without questioning My timing and precision.
Her heart was designed after Mine,
To love the people, tell them about Me, and fight the front lines.
As your life goes on My daughter and you begin to seek a mate,
Remember I loved you first.
Don't go before Me,
My plan for you awaits.

CHAPTER 10

Don't Forget God When You Get What You Prayed For

When the time comes and you receive what God has promised to you, I want to leave you with one piece of advice. Do not forget Him when you cross into the promised land. There was an instruction given to the Israelites in Joshua 4 that when they crossed over the Jordan River they were to set up twelve stones as a memorial to what God had done that day. This was requested so when the future generations passed by, they would not forget the miracle that took place.

Sometimes we forget the Lord once we've received what we wanted from Him. We begin to worship the promise and forget to worship the Master. See, we've begged and waited and pleaded so long that once we receive it we forget Him. We only sought after Him for this house, this job, this healing, this husband, this baby, and eventually stopped seeking *Him* just to know *Him*. In various seasons I have been guilty of this.

God deserves your attention and affection even when He isn't handing out everything we ask for. God deserves our time even when nothing seems to be changing in our circumstance. God is more than a vending machine, and we must be careful to remember that.

> I know your works, your labor, your patience, and that you cannot bear those who are evil. And you have tested those who say they are apostles and are not, and have found them liars; and you have persevered and have patience, and have labored for My name's sake and have not become weary. Nevertheless I have this against you, that you have left your first love. Remember therefore from where you have fallen; repent and do the first works, or else I will come to you quickly and remove your lampstand from its place—unless you repent (Revelation 2:2-5).

You. Left. Your. First. Love.

Imagine. To leave Jesus. After all that time. After all the prayers. To simply walk away. Imagine being so enamored with this life that we neglect our eternal life.

Imagine being so caught up in what we don't have, we forget what was done.

Don't leave your first love.

Be cautious not to idolize the promise in your life. Sometimes we place people on a pedestal and exalt them. Sometimes we exalt circumstances rather than exalting Him. Remember when Hannah finally had a child? She dedicated him back to the Lord. See, she knew where her gift had come from. She did not forget God after He blessed her.

It's very easy to get busy once you meet the one God had for you. You're spending all of your time with him, you're on the phone constantly, you're going here and there with him, and you're distracted by thoughts of him. Maybe you're even planning your wedding! All of that is wonderful; you have waited for this and now it's finally here. *But* do not forget *He* who gave him to you. Do not forget the God who hand made that husband just for you. Do not forget the God who turned your situation around and confounded the doctors by giving you a child. Do not forget the God who picked you up out of the mess that you were in and changed your life.

Do not forget your first love.

Even I was guilty of this. There were times being engaged that I turned my husband into an idol. It wasn't his fault; he never asked that of me. But because I was so excited and so happy, I didn't even realize I had walked away from my relationship with the Lord. I had stopped spending those countless hours in worship and prayer, and it started to show. I pray that you keep your priorities straight when you step into your promised land.

In the Bible, we see an example of this. When Jesus healed ten lepers of their disease, only one returned to praise Him.

> So Jesus answered and said, "Were there not ten cleansed? But where are the [other] nine? Were there not any found who returned to give glory to God except this foreigner? (Luke 17:17-18).

I caution you, be the one who comes back and testifies of what the Lord has done. Be the one who never stops giving Him glory. Be the one who praises Him in the harvest. The healing is great, the baby is great, the husband is great, and all of these things are generously given miracles. However, they will never satisfy your spirit like He who performed that miracle.

As you enter into a new season of your life, make sure you are giving honor where it is due. God was there for you when nobody else was. God bottled every tear, heard every cry, and carefully curated your needs and desires as He answered you. God was faithful to you; now it is your turn to remain faithful to Him. Don't lose your prayer life now that you have what you asked for. Don't stop fasting. Don't stop showing up to every service. Abide in Him. Your life will not be perfect after you get married; you will need God even more. The trials won't end after you receive the promise. Stay close to Him, and remember *He* loved you first.

I waited patiently for the Lord; and He inclined to me, and heard my cry. He also brought me up out of a horrible pit, out of the miry clay, and set my feet upon a rock, and established my steps. He has put a new song in my mouth—praise to our God; many will see it and fear, and will trust in the Lord. Blessed is that man who makes the Lord his trust, and does not respect the proud, nor such as turn aside to lies. Many, O Lord my God, are Your wonderful works which You have done; and Your thoughts toward us cannot be recounted to You in order; if I would declare and speak of them, they are more than can be numbered (Psalm 40:1-5).

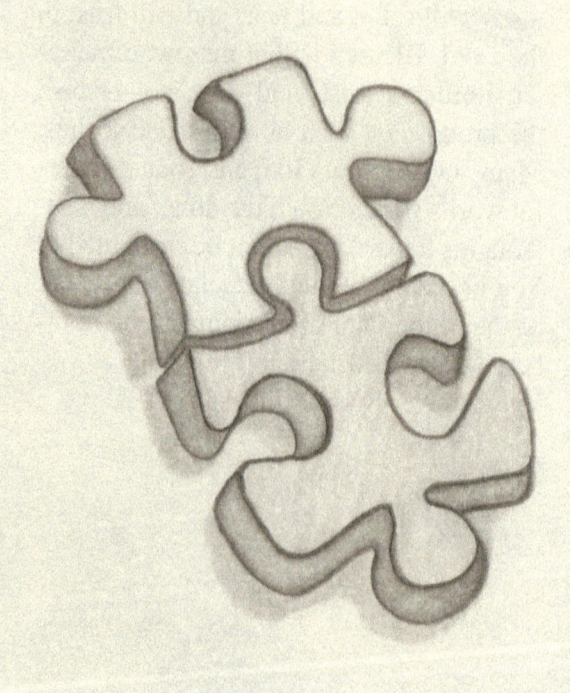

Afterword

This book is a collection of lessons I have been taught in my waiting season. As I look back over my life, I see the hand of God in every moment. Every slammed door was His protection. Every "No" was for my good. Every hurt and disappointment gave me a greater hope and expectation for His plan. Every heartache only made me more grateful when I received His promise. How do I say thank You, Lord?

I want you to know that I have thought, fought, and toiled on the last chapters of this book. I have tried in my own spirit to wrap this up in a way that would apply to any waiting room that you find yourself in. I pondered using the natural seasons as inspiration, and I thought I figured it out. But as weeks and then months went by, I had no true inspiration or clarity on those topics. Then, I realized I was trusting in my own ability to complete this book. After praying and stressing one morning, I opened the Word and began to read 2 Kings. As I began to study Elisha's ministry on that Friday morning at the end of September, I had a breakthrough. The Lord gave me this particular question: What are *you* waiting for?

In answering His question, I began to realize that even now, I'm in the waiting. I have a thyroid condition that I am waiting on the Lord to heal. Prior to this writing this book, I was waiting on the direction of the Lord in ministry. And then I realized that I am waiting on Him *always*. The wait is not a temporary season; it is the roll of the waves in life. We will always need Him for something. As we *wait* upon the Lord, we learn to trust in His timing, our faith builds, and we grow more in love with the Father.

Now having received, I see the purpose behind the wait. I see that nothing I ever went through was for me; it was to share with you, my friend. Every season brought wisdom and gave me something to pass along to you. I have given you all that I have for now, except my testimony.

My testimony is Ephesians 3:20, "Now to Him who is able to [carry out His purpose and] do superabundantly more than all that we dare ask or think [infinitely beyond our greatest prayers, hopes, or dreams], according to His power that is at work within us" (AMP). God has exceeded every hope, every dream, and every prayer. Let me elaborate.

When I was 16, in 2017, I was in the car with my mom and my Aunt Ellen. As we slowed for a red light, my aunt began to tell me God had shown her the back of my husband's head. I was upset because that didn't seem like a lot of detail to me then. She described his height as tall, hair color as dark, a style which was "different," and skin tone as tan. I hid these descriptions in my heart and continued to wait, knowing what God says is final.

Then in the winter of 2019, my Aunt Dianne prophesied a word over my life. She spoke that what I had been waiting for was coming "quickly." Later that day she reiterated it and gave me an explanation of what that meant. She said that it will happen quickly, as in it's going to be done soon. She referenced the scripture where Jesus said, "Behold, I am coming quickly." She meant from the time the relationship begins it will unfold quickly and all the events, such as dating, engagement, and the wedding, will happen very fast.

God's faithfulness continued to be revealed as He dropped pieces of hope in place and strung my story together as a friend of mine approached me in the summer of 2020. She reached out and gave me a necklace that read "Suddenly." She said that she didn't know what that meant to me, but that the Lord instructed her to give it to me. Little did she know, I was waiting on a "quickly" and a "suddenly" from God.

Furthermore, while I waited, I asked God for a very short, specific list of the characteristics my husband would have. These are some of the qualities for which I prayed: a kind and gentle spirit, not arrogant or rude, a loving heart, spiritually supportive, fun, adventurous, gorgeous eyes, honest, compassionate, a great conversationalist, loves me as I am (despite my flaws), loves my family, and one who would pursue me boldly, with no hesitation.

I finally met my soon-to-be husband in 2021. Just as my Aunt Ellen described him in the car that day several years ago, Sam is 6 feet 5 inches, very tan skin, with long, dark curly hair; his eyes are a stunning ice blue. He has a unique look that makes him stand out in a crowd, and he is different than anyone I'd ever seen before. Late that year in December, I was in church with Sam, and my Aunt Ellen approached he and I. She placed my hand on top of his and began to tell us that God had ordained us to be together before we were even born. She looked at him and back to me with a smile as if to say, "This is who I saw." Two weeks later we were engaged.

God kept His promise. I can testify that every single thing on that list is who my husband is. My husband marched into a room full of women the day that we met, and we talked for four hours. That was a big deal for him because he was somewhat shy. From that day forward we were all but inseparable. He didn't make me question or wonder what his intentions were. He was persistent and didn't waste any of my time. From the time we met until we were engaged was seven months. And seven months later we were married. The Lord took my request for a man who would pursue me boldly with no hesitation very seriously and He delivered. It was a whirlwind. It was "suddenly' and it was "quickly" and it was beautiful.

Was every day easy? No. Was every day normal? No. Was God's hand on us every step of the way? Yes! Did God orchestrate every moment? Yes!

Often, we emphasize the wait. I fell for that too. Stop considering the wait so much, because you will find yourself on a man-made clock. Live. Live for Jesus. Don't sell yourself short looking for love in the world. Let Him love you first, and He will lead the right person to you. Do not allow what you see to make you doubt what God said. When you devote your life and surrender your will to Him, He will write you a love story that will put famous romance novelists out of business. He doesn't leave out one detail or a missing piece. When God promises you something, hold on to it, and don't settle for anything less.

As we walk through life, we find ourselves waiting on different things. Some are waiting on a spouse. Some are waiting for a child. Some are waiting for healing. Some are waiting for restoration. Some are waiting on deliverance. Some are waiting for a financial breakthrough. The key to solving *all* of these circumstances is Jesus.

> Concerning this thing I pleaded with the Lord three times that it might depart from me. And He said to me, "My grace is sufficient for you, for My strength is made perfect in weakness." Therefore most gladly I will rather boast in my infirmities, that the power of Christ may rest upon me (2 Corinthians 12:8-9).

His. Grace. Is. Sufficient.

He is *more* than able.

He is *Jehovah*.

But who are you calling on? There were many instances in the Bible when He was referred to by a different name. Jehovah Jireh, Jehovah Nissi, Jehovah Rapha, Jehovah

Shalom, Jehovah Shammah, El Roi, and many more. No matter how you refer to Him, He is personal. He meets you where you are, and I want you to remember that.

He isn't just God when everything is perfect, He is God when nothing makes sense. He is God when everything is falling apart. He is God when you're on the mountain, and He's God when you're in a valley. He is your creator, and He knows what you need. So, my friend, I will ask you this: What are you waiting for?

Don't accept a counterfeit version of who God has promised you. Do not accept the Ishmael; wait on the Isaac. Don't compromise your standards or your heart's desires out of impatience. Every single prayer, God answers! Every single tear, He bottles. Your wait is not in vain. He will not forget you or break His promises. Delve into His goodness and rest in His presence. Embrace His essence and *know* that He is God.

And most importantly wait, *wait* on the Master's time.

> Not a word failed of any good thing which
> the Lord had spoken to the house of Israel.
> All came to pass (Joshua 21:45).

Look daughter, now you see,
I AM the God of exceedingly and abundantly.
I went beyond your expectations
And surpassed your dreams,
While you were praying
I was working behind the scenes.
I kept My word and My promises rang true,
You're glad you didn't give up on Me, aren't you?
All of those times you didn't understand
You cried pleading for Me to hurry up,
Not knowing that the timing was planned.
While you were praying
I was busy doing my best,
While you were praying
I was busy doing the rest.
I was moving the pieces and connecting the dots,
My plan was much greater than you thought.
See while you were praying
I was leading both of you,
I had a plan that neither of you knew.
I never leave anything incomplete or undone,
But you haven't seen anything yet daughter,
Your story has just begun.
I have more in store for you two, just wait and see
For I am the God of exceedingly and abundantly.

About the Author

Paige Cooper grew up serving in her home church, Cornerstone Faith Assembly in Richmond, Virginia.

After marriage to Sam Cooper she moved to Denton, Maryland where she and her husband currently serve and worship at Living Waters Assembly.

Paige's heart's desire is to win souls to the kingdom and to see God's people living their lives confidently, knowing that He who started a good work is able to complete it. (Phil. 1:6). Her life is dedicated to serving God and His people.

On the Masters Time is Paige's first title. She can be contacted at paigecooper.ptc@gmail.com.